FORWARD

Of all the "Student Teachers" I've mentored over the years, Robin Johnson stands head & shoulders above all others as the most persistent and success driven, bar none!

From overcoming neglect and sexual abuse as a child to rising above it all and going on to inspire others in a profound and meaningful way.

Let Robin's personal story told in this most sensitive & poignant way, illustrate what courage and a passion for helping others can do, in redefining and altering one's life's script.

Mel Brodsky

Jazzy Kitty Publications Presents

I'M STILL STANDING
Gone through the Storms of Life
To the Rainbow of Victories

ROBIN JOHNSON

I'm Still Standing

Gone Through the Storms of Life to the Rainbow of Victories

By Robin D. Johnson

Cover Created and Designed By: Jazzy Kitty Publications
Cover Photograph: Kelly De'Anne Mobley/Sync Me Studio
Logo Designs: Andre M. Saunders
Editor: Anelda L. Attaway

© 2018 Robin D. Johnson
ISBN 978-0-9988433-8-4
Library of Congress Control Number: 2017953716

All rights reserved. This book is protected by the copyright laws of the United States of America. This book may not be copied or reprinted for commercial gain or profit. The use of short quotations or occasional page copying for personal or group study is permitted and encouraged. Permission will be granted upon request. For Worldwide Distribution, available in Paperback and eBook. Printed in the United States of America. Published by Jazzy Kitty Greetings Marketing & Publishing, LLC dba Jazzy Kitty Publications (Formerly Jazzy Kitty Publishing). Utilizing Microsoft Publishing Software.

ACKNOWLEDGMENTS

First and foremost, I thank God and my Savior Jesus the Christ. For He had my spirit with Him from the beginning and sent my spirit here on earth. God kept me here for a reason and has kept me safe from harm. He continues each day to protect my body, soul, and spirit.

To Dorothy J Gross, my mother. She raised me as a single parent and did what she had to do for me to survive. She may not be on this earth today; I thank God for having a mother like her. I wanted her to see me reach my dreams and goals, I hoped one day I can pay her back in the next life for some of her sacrifice she did for me. Thanks to Rev. and Mrs. Thomas Moon for their part in my life, Rev. Moon for helping me when I gave my life to Christ in 1988.

To my children, Samuel E. Davis Jr. and Tamera D. Davis. My children are a true blessing to me. They never have given me any real trouble and I know they do love me. My children are a special blessing from God. My son who is 39 became a Deacon at his former church. Raising a Black son by myself wasn't easy but had God on my side. Tamera, who is 22 is currently attending Lincoln University College.

To my Bishop, David G. Evans of Bethany Baptist Church located in Lindenwold, NJ. Thank you, Bishop for all the teachings and the love you have shown your Church Members. Thank you for being there for me and my daughter when we needed you. 13 years under your teachings Bishop have been a blessing to me. Also, Pastor Nick for your teachings. Thank God for both of you!!!

To my friend, business colleague Dwain Smith, who is no longer here on this earth was a true friend; you have helped me with the business even when your health was not great. You were a great mentor and teacher in helping me to succeed. I will miss you dearly.

To my Mentor Mel Brodsky from California, you are a great mentor and friend to me. To have met you July 2002 at a Networking Event in Maryland was a true blessing; you always seem to be there for me when I really needed you and you always had the right words to encourage me at the right time. God as bless me with a true friend.

Lastly, thank you to my publisher Anelda L. Attaway of Jazzy Kitty Publications for her continued support, dedication, and hard work.

DEDICATIONS

This book is dedicated in memory to my mother the Late Dorothy J. Gross.

This book is also dedicated to all readers that have a testimony to share with others. I thank God for giving me the vision to write a story that I believe will help many and all types of people.

TABLE OF CONTENTS

INTRODUCTION i

CHAPTER 1 – Why Do I Feel Left Out? 01
   Poem 05

CHAPTER 2 – Narrow Path 07
   Poem 10

CHAPTER 3 – In the Midst of It All 12
   Poem 14

CHAPTER 4 – Why Me? 16
   Poem 18

CHAPTER 5 – Healing in the Sorrows 21
   Poem 24

CHAPTER 6 – I Belong to You 26
   Poem 28

CHAPTER 7 – Down in the Valley 30
   Poem 32

CHAPTER 8 – Prosperity 33
   Poem 37

INSPIRATIONAL POETRY 39
   A Dreamer 40
   Growing up Like This as a Child 42
   The Little Boy 43
   The Little Girl 45
   Father's Day 47
   Who Can Define a Man? 48
   Who Can Define a Woman? 50

TABLE OF CONTENTS

A Husband, a Wife 52

My Love 54

Natural Love, Spiritual Love 56

Girlfriend 58

What Is a Friend? 59

Peace 60

Respect 63

My Brother Why Kill Another? 64

Soul Brother 66

Satisfies 68

Live for Today 69

Christian, I Am, Christian, I Will Be 71

The Precious Gift 72

Look to the Hills 73

Restored 75

Yesterday Is Gone 76

ABOUT THE AUTHOR 78

INTRODUCTION

Praise be to God and Jesus Christ, my Lord and Savior. The pages in this book will reflect on my life from childhood to adulthood. Yes, this book is about me, but my purpose is to bless others by giving them hope when they feel they can't go on in life.

My name is Robin D. Johnson and I was born on June 25, 1961, in Wilmington Delaware. I was raised by a single parent, my mother the Late Dorothy J. Gross and she worked two jobs to provide for me. She may not have been around as much as I would have liked, but she had to do what was necessary to take care of me.

As I begin to write my thoughts on paper, I look back and thank God, I'm still here today in 2018 with God watching over me and having the Blood of Jesus Christ protecting me. I believe my life is where it should be; safe and fulfilling my destiny and dreams.

CHAPTER 1

Why Do I Feel Left Out? Who Am I?

The day is Tuesday, March 3, 2009, and this is the day that the Lord has made and I shall rejoice and be glad in it. I like to begin with my childhood. I was born on June 25, 1961 in Wilmington Delaware to the Late Dorothy C. Johnson (Gross). My mother did what she could to raise me right without a father. As a child growing up on the Eastside of Wilmington, it was hard sometimes being the only child and not having a lot of friends was somewhat difficult. I never really had a childhood, meaning being by myself due to kids picking on me and being bullied. I never understood why this happened, but I made it through. *I ask myself why this happening to me?* Even today kids are being treated unfairly and bullied. I hope one day I will receive the answer.

One year while attending elementary school, I was attacked in front of the school. A young male threw me up against the fence and tried to rape me. Here I was, only 8-years-old and someone was that evil to attack a young girl. Today, I believe one of God's angels were watching over me because my mother came out in time and stopped me from being raped. Until this day, he has not been caught or charged for this vicious crime.

My childhood was strange, what I mean is, I was a nice little girl and I did my best to treat everyone nicely, but for some reason, kids did not like me. I was talked about, spit on, and hit on by girls and boys. This was hard because I never was taught how to protect myself. My family or friends were not around to help me. I felt lonely as a child not knowing what to do in this situation. When a girl has no father in their life, it can have a profound effect on her. Due to not having a father and feeling so alone, I ended up hanging with the wrong crowd of people and doing things that were not right or good for me. Growing up like this shouldn't happen to any child.

Today in 2018; there are so many children growing up without a father in their home, no mentor or a real role model to help single parent's. But I thank God that my mother was my role model and her love was pure and awesome. Love is important to a child's development in life and without love, we will make bad choices and head down the wrong path in life. I know some obstacles and challenges are to help make us stronger, but for a young girl or boy, I feel this should happen later in life.

It's important to choose the right friends as a child because it can affect you in the long run. When I was a teenager there was a young lady who was a lot older than me in the old neighborhood. She finds out that I was seeing her ex-boyfriend and he was a lot older than I was. Therefore, the lady was in the process of telling my mother. But before she said anything, she told me if I gave her money she wouldn't tell. Not knowing this was considered blackmail and that I could have reported her to the police. Because I didn't have any loyal friends to help me or anyone to guide me besides my mother, I didn't know anything about blackmail. My mother did the best she could; she worked two jobs to take care of me. Even though she worked a lot, she was able to instill great values in me that I cherish and I love her for that. Most importantly, my mother gave me the best gift of all; she gave me the opportunity to know the Lord Jesus Christ my Savior. Now getting back regarding the young lady who blackmailed me, and YES! I did give her the money she wanted. Today I am alive in 2018 and the lady passed away in the 1990's. I believe we will reap what we sow, treat people right and love one another so our days on this earth can be very long. Now, I'm not saying

I'm Still Standing

I was a perfect little girl, but I did do my best to treat people with likeness and love. At the age of eight, I was molested by a family member at a family member's house. Till this day, I don't know why this happened to me, but who knows why everything happens to them. I'm 56 today and I will take this unpleasant experience to my grave or when my Lord and Savior comes for me. If someone had walked in on this, would the family believe me or him? That's the million-dollar question.

Even though this happened to me, I still love that family member and I forgave him. I just hope God will have mercy on his soul. I hope this part of the book will let others who have gone through this will be able to forgive the person who treated them dirty, made them feel worthless, and/or feeling it was their fought. Things like this are still happening today after 48 years of this happening to me. The United States must make Child Molestation Laws a more severe punishment. That is why molestation is high and happens often. In other countries, the punishment is so severe; that is why the crime rate is very low.

Life can be happy, sad, perfect, and challenging. And in reality, life is NOT perfect. However, with Jesus Christ, you will have happiness, perfect peace, and long-suffering for getting the victory at the end.

Now, I look back on my childhood today and I thank God for being there, watching my back, and keeping me safe through the trials and tribulations. God already knows that the wrong people would come into my life. He had a reason for allowing me to go through those challenging times. In fact, it made me stronger today to endure the things I'm dealing with now.

Sitting here typing this, I just remembered about a friend in middle school who I thought was a real friend but wasn't. She allowed things to go unpunished, by that I mean, a family member slapped me and she didn't do anything about it. She disrespected me and just treated me like an enemy.

Again, I'm not perfect until I'm with Jesus, but I did not deserve being bullied as a child or teenager.

I know God has a special place for me here on earth and in His Kingdom. You know Jesus is the Best Friend a person can have. He will treat you with love, respect, and keep you in perfect peace.

Now that I understand the true meaning of a friend, I'm making better choices in life choosing my friends. What is a devoted friend? A person who cares about you and not what you can do for them. A friend is being there if you need someone to talk to. If you're hungry and they have extra food to help you until you get back on your feet. A friend that will not judge you or look down on you because you don't have a lot of possessions. They are not concerned with the kind of car you drive, but the kind of heart you have. What if you don't have a car? Then the friend will offer to take you to church with them and even to the store. The bottom line is, <u>a friend</u> will be there until the end.

Keep in mind the best friend you have is Jesus Christ your Savior.

Jeremiah, Chapter 1 Verse 4-5

Then the Word of the Lord came to me saying: Before I formed you in the womb I knew you; Before you were born I sanctified you; I ordained you a prophet to the nations.

WHY DO I FEEL LEFT OUT?
WHO AM I?

WHO AM I?

You say I am a Young Lady Just Passing Thru

But **WHO AM I**, where do I Belong?

On the side of the road, I Stand

And Watch the cars go by

Sometimes I Smile has people look my way,

Some Smile back but most just Stare

I ask,

"Am I strange for sharing joy and for wanting

My Love to Shine?"

Am I left out in the Cold, does anyone Understand me?

Can you relate to **FEELING LEFT OUT?**

Family so Far away, Communication to No Avail

Friends are few, Acquaintance many

I feel NO Love. . .Why is that?

Am I Passing Thru the Wrong Time?
Am I to be Here, what is my Call?

I know a Man who wasn't Loved, by many
He fought for My Love Just Passing thru,
But He took the time to say I Love You

Is it Strange wanting Love from Near and Far?
Sharing Hugs and Kisses that come from Above

WHO AM I?

AM I LEFT OUT

OR WILL I JUST KEEP PASSING THRU?

CHAPTER 2

Narrow Path

This chapter demonstrates the beginning of my teenage years, the bad choices I've made, and the ones that were beyond my control. The year was 1975 and I was in high school. While in school, I mainly stayed to myself, not really reaching out to have friends. However, there was one student who did become a friend of mind. She was my "get hi" friend. We smoked marijuana on our lunch break. I felt that doing this would help be more of a friendly person in school, meaning make more friends. I found out that this was the wrong way to make friends. In the 11th grade I felt alone and not doing well with my grades, but doing okay, enough to pass my classes.

In June 1978, at the age of 17 I found out that I was pregnant. The father was someone I started seeing at the age of 15. I knew that I should have waited to have sex until I was out of school and married. But because I wanted to be grown before time and I did not make good decisions. However, I did finish high school and I married the father of my son. My son was a true blessing from God. The sin is in the sex and not the baby growing inside of you.

I stayed married to this man for only one year and it ended because he was abusing me. He punched me in the mouth which messed up my front teeth and he also punched me in the stomach when I was carrying his child. I realized, in life we need to listen to our mind, our heart, and put trust in our God.

In July of 1978, this man hit me in the face. I thought then it was a love tap. That was a sign not to marry this man and get away from him. Even though I was pregnant with his child this should not have been a reason to stay with him.

On November 11, 1978, my wedding day, I took sick and almost didn't make it to the ceremony. My aunt told me not to go, but I didn't listen. Today, I believe that this was God's way of trying to stop me from making bad choices. This man beat on me for about a year. I even went to counseling to help him, but this didn't help at all. Time went by and he would stalk me, tried to take my son, and he threw me on top of a car. I'm thankful that God had my back and was watching over me.

During the year, I was married to my son's father and I know it was a learning experience for me. In 1979, around the summer I went to the house I used to live with my son's father. I remember going to get something for my son. When I got there my ex-was there and you would not believe what he did. He would not let me leave the house. He grabbed my arm and took my son. He said I couldn't have my son back unless I had sex with him. Who would have thought a man would do this to his son's mother? He threw me on the bed and raped me while my one-year-old son watches from the crib that was left in the house.

I tell this story to say to other women that may be in an abusive relationship, get out! Don't stay because of children or you think this is the only man you may have in your life. Women look for signs when you're dating a man. Most of all, talk to God and ask Him is this your soulmate, someone who will treat you like a Queen. Always believe that you are special in God's sight, and you deserve a man that will treat you special.

After all, this took place I moved back in with my mother. I was looking for a job and I went on public assistance until I found work. I was only on public assistance for six months. I found a job to take care of my son and me. I may have had to struggle for a while, but I refused to give up and let my ex-husband win.

Even though I let this man do this to me, I made the mistake of marrying him, so I forgave him. This forgiveness was not for him, but for me. God says we must forgive our enemies. The blessing that came out of this troubled relationship was my son who is now 39-years-old and doing very well.

As I write about my life I think about the movie Forrest Gump. *Life is like a box of chocolate you never know what you're going get.* Life has its challenges, but we have the strength that the Lord gives us to fight and survive.

Habakkuk Chapter 3 Verse 19, NKJV

The Lord God is my strength; He will make my feet like deer's feet, And He will make me walk on my high hills.

NARROW PATH

As I Walk down the **PATH**
On a Sunny Day,
I say to Myself
Thank You, Lord, for this Day

Am I Walking on the **RIGHT PATH** of my Life?
Am I Headed for Trouble down the Road?

When I Trip off the **PATH,**
Do I Fall or Catch myself. . .
Before Hitting the Ground?

What **PATH** am I really on?

The **WIDE PATH** with so much Destruction,
The **PATH** of Sickness
Or the **PATH** of Sin?

The **NARROW PATH** consists of
Wisdom, Love, and Peace within yourself

So, I ask Myself,

Which **PATH** do I want to be on?

THE ANSWER IS SIMPLE,

The **PATH** that will lead Me

To Everlasting Life

A life with Joy, Peace, and Happiness

To God be the Glory,

And My Lord and Savior Jesus Christ

CHAPTER 3

In the Midst of It All

The perfect life, nobody on earth has a perfect life. What I mean is sometimes we all make mistakes, bad decisions, and treat people wrong. Today, I know I was nowhere near perfect. I made a lot of bad decisions and I was not the woman that God wanted me to be.

After the breakup with my ex my son's father, I started going out to clubs, doing drugs, and drinking alcohol. This was a choice I made, no one else. A gun was not pointed to my head. I believed going to clubs every night and dating different men was a way of filling a void in my life. Not having a father to love me, friends, and family members to be with hurt me more than I could have imagined.

In 1982, I made a real mistake at the age of 21, I started shoplifting in groceries stores. I was stealing meats and other items. I got caught one day stealing small items worth about 5 dollars. Because of this, I almost went to jail, but again I was spared. I paid a $50 fine and was on probation for two months'. Even though I knew this was wrong, I still tried to get away with it. Getting caught is what help me to stop and I give God the praise for this. From all the hurt in life, I knew there had to be a better life out there for me.

In April 1988, Resurrection Sunday, I gave my life to my Lord and Savior Jesus Christ. I was Baptist Christian and I received the Holy Spirit "The Comforter" seeing doves ascending in the sky. Once I accepted Christ, I knew my life would change. I went through trials and tribulations to make me the woman I am today. I may get weary sometimes, but I will always fight and never give up on making my life what God wants it to be.

Receiving the Lord in my life at the age of 26 was a huge step for me.

Even though I was learning about the Lord, I was still making bad decisions. Receiving God in your heart, body, and soul is not easy. You must learn how to pray for yourself and others. Also, how to forgive one another for any wrongdoings.

God gives us second chances every day, so we can grow closer to Him. The one thing I had trouble with stopping was looking to have a man in my life. I was looking in the wrong places and I was still trying to feel a void of not having a father in my life.

This decision caused me to still do drugs, party in clubs all the time, and date the wrong type of men. But my God was still working with me. This is the kind of God He is, a merciful and loving true God. Now, I know that all things in my life have a purpose here on earth.

**ature*I John, Chapter 1 Verse 9, NKJV*

If we confess our sins, He is faithful and just to forgive us our sins and to cleanse us from all unrighteousness.

IN THE MIDST OF IT ALL

IN THE MIDST OF IT ALL,

The Water Rush thru the Sea

The Sun so Bright, the Sky So Clear,

At Night, the Stars are Glowing

The Moon Pure and White,

IN THE MIDST OF IT ALL

The Sky becomes Dark,

The Sun Shines NO MORE,

And the Sky is Oh So Dark

In my Christian Walk,

The Holy Spirit Rushes

My Eyes LIGHT UP like

The Stars from Above

My Heart Pure like the Moon

I am Cleanse from my Sins

White as Snow

When I Fall off the Path,

My face NO GLOW,

My eyes filled with Fear

And my Heart gets Heavy

When all is said and done,

My Lord is with me on this Journey,

And He is Carrying me

ALL THE WAY

CHAPTER 4

Why Me?

This was the time of my life where things started looking like my life was over. Meaning, I thought that God had forgotten about me. My dreams and goals weren't coming fast enough for me. I thought because I received the Lord in my life, that everything would immediately change. This is not true and now my faith is being tested. God didn't leave me, He was carrying me through my trials and tribulations. Life is very challenging and sometimes scary, but with the Lord on my side nothing can harm me.

In 1990, around the summer I started dealing with depression. I heard of depression and the signs, but never thought I would be dealing with this illness. I think back to 1984 when I was going through some tough times and staying in the house a lot. I wouldn't good to work, eat, and got no sleep. I was about to commit suicide and give my son to my mother. I was going to put myself in the State Hospital for psychiatric help. Somehow, I pulled myself out and kept my son with me. Not knowing that I was dealing with depression then, but the Lord knew and He kept me here for His purpose.

In 1990, I started seeing more signs of depression, I was getting angry a lot and staying shut down in the house. I lost jobs, stop talking with friends, and family. I was ready to give up on life. For some reason, I just couldn't take my life.

It's funny when you think this is just about you, but life isn't just for you. Life is a testimonial to others who may be experiencing things only a loving person can help them with. What I'm saying is, a person who cares about people no matter what the color of their skin, what type of house they have, or their background. A person who has the love of God in them. I pray this book about my life will bless many people around the world.

For many years (about 18), I was dealing with this illness. I always thought I could fix it myself. Sometimes people feel they don't need anyone's help in this world. This is not true, we all need good people in our lives and someone to truly love us to the fullest.

During the 1990s, I was dealing with the challenge of trying to fix my problems with depression. I was going to church, praying to my Lord and Savior, and working on my salvation to stay on the right path. I didn't think I needed any kind of help but the Lords, this isn't true. God gives us a place to go for help like your pastor and church family, and/or a mentor. We may think our Spirit is all we need, but we still must take care of this shell our Spirit lives in.

As I conclude Chapter IV, I want to say to those that are experiencing these same issues, I beg you to get help. Don't let the Enemy win by taking your life and not fulfilling your goals and dreams.

Isaiah, Chapter 43 Verse 2, NKJV

When you pass through the waters, I will be with you; And through the rivers, they shall not overflow you.

WHY ME?

I planned my Future to be Successful,

But what am I to be?

Days are Long, Nights are Short,

And Struggles are Surround me

I look in the Mirror

And what do I see?

A Woman in her 40s

A Single Mom,

And I ask **WHY ME?**

Love is in my Heart, Humble I try to be,

Mistakes, YES, a few Lessons Learned

Yet, I still Yearned to ask myself

WHY ME?

When will the Struggles End?

How can I Chase the Obstacles away?

Visions I Write, Seeds I Plant,

Harvest Time YET NOT SEEN

Is life Fair or Unfair?

What is my PURPOSE on this Earth?

Is it to Love or Hate?

Is it to be Rich or Poor,

Do I even know?

Oh, the Struggles I have in my Life

And I say **WHY ME?**

The Struggles make me Stronger;

I turn to my Creator for Strength

Love can make me Smile,

Sometimes even Laugh

Mistakes help me to Grow

From being Poor to being Rich

For God gave me His Son Jesus Christ

That when I look in the Mirror,

I can say **WHY ME?**

BECAUSE I HAVE THE VICTORY!

CHAPTER 5

Healing in the Sorrows

It was the year of 2000 around May and I moved to the state of Virginia. There is where I found a networking business called LegalShield Inc. This business really changed my life. I met a lot of great people and found good mentors. I have always wanted to have my own business that would help people. The Lord says to wait on Him and He will direct your paths.

I moved to Virginia not knowing what kind of job I would get. I started working for a time share company located in Virginia Beach, one of my co-workers introduced me to LegalShield Inc. I've been in business for myself, but not by myself for 17 years.

Things were going great until my car was hit and I became homeless. My 4-year-old daughter and I had to stay in a hotel. All my belongings were in my car where we almost had to sleep. Thank the Lord we didn't. I think about people who live on the streets every day and here I was only homeless for three months. I know I would not have been able to live on the streets like other people. I don't know how the homeless make it every day. I pray that God keeps them safe and eventually there will be no more homelessness in the future.

After being in VA for 6 months, I moved back to Delaware and moved into a nice townhome. Thanks be to God for blessing me with a roof over my head. My business was doing well and I found my passion regarding a career.

Now you would think I would have learned my lesson after my car accident in 1984, but I didn't. In 2002, I was leaving an event in Virginia with my daughter and a colleague of mind. I knew I was tired, but I wanted to get back to Delaware. I know God had my angels with me because I fell asleep at the wheel five times. Amazingly, I had no accident or brought harm to anyone on the road that night. Each time I fell asleep I felt a hand on my chest. This had to be my angel waking me up. I still was being hard headed because I didn't pull over to take a quick nap. I could have killed my daughter and colleague, but thanks be to God we made it back to Delaware safely. I tell this part of my life to say listen to your inner Spirit to know when to pull over or not even drive a car.

One day I started asking for help with depression. The reason I asked for help was because I was in the house for three months in a row. This was June of 2008 to August 2008. I first called my church and I spoke to a minister that worked in this area. I was evaluated by the minister and she took an intake on me. The next thing I was told to seek my doctor immediately. I went to my family doctor and was checked out for symptoms of depression. I was then put on medication. Also, my doctor had me to get therapy. I found a good therapist here in the New Castle area of Delaware. I started therapy August 2008 and I'm still faithfully in therapy to this day. The medication started working and I was somewhat balanced, but in December of 2008 I had a relapse. I shut down again for a month.

I went back to my family doctor and she immediately sent me to the emergency room at Christiana Hospital in Delaware because I was having suicidal thoughts again. I was evaluated in the psychiatric area of the hospital. After the evaluation, I was sent to the Wilmington Hospital Psychiatric Department and I was told I should stay overnight. I refused to stay, therefore, I was put in the outpatient program. I fought the program for the first week because I didn't want to be in the program. I thought my Spirit would eventually fix my problem. Now, I know that the Spirit is in a shell made of flesh and God has given men and women the gift to take care of the flesh when it's ill. Due to living on this earth we breathe in all types of chemicals from the air and chemicals that are put on our foods can have an influence on our bodies.

The Lord has given me a gift of knowing when I must trust Him. Even though the pain in my life can be hard sometimes, I must trust God with all my heart, my soul, my body, and my mind. Writing this part of the book is my testimonial that with all things trust God.

Proverbs Chapter 3, Verse 5-6, NKJV

Trust in the Lord with all your heart, and lean not on your own understanding; In all your ways acknowledge Him, And He shall direct your paths.

HEALING IN THE SORROWS

HEALED in the Morning,

HEALED in the Afternoon

Scars I have. . .

Oh, the Pain I've Endured

HEALED in the Evening,

Prayer is ALL I HAVE

Is there a **HEALING** for the Scars?

The Balm of **HEALING**

Seems So Far

The Attributes of Love covering the Pain

Exercising my Faith is ALL I HAVE

Pass Scars keep me in the Bondage,

The Present Loosens the Chains

Unconditional Love from Above

Removing my Scars

So, I can Soar above the Stars

Submerged I'll be

As Deep as the Sea

For the Future is Bright

And Will Set Me Free

CHAPTER 6

I Belong to You

In the midst of dealing with depression, now knowing that I was diagnosed with Bipolar and I will have a long road ahead. What I mean is my faith is being tested and my trust in God. Today I'm still taking my medications and seeing my therapist as needed. I have some days that are hard and I have mood changes once in a blue moon. And thanks be to God, I have been delivered from the crying spells and anger issues. Even with this illness, I still trust my Lord Jesus Christ. I know He's by my side and carrying me through this storm of my life. My Spirit is intact and my faith is stronger than it's ever been. This is due to reading God's Word, studying His Word, and believing what His Word says. God's Word is the blueprint for our lives.

During this time of my life around March 2009, I had an MRI done and found that I had small marks on my brain. This could have come from a car accident that took place 1984. The accident was my fault due to not paying attention. I was eating while driving and I had been drinking alcohol. I was 22-years-old at the time. I'm grateful I don't drink anymore, do drugs, or smoke cigarettes. There is a time in everybody's life you should decide to change for the better. If we don't look at our life and see there are things we can change about ourselves, we will always make bad choices that can have a long-term effect.

I have one chance here on earth to have my dreams and goals to be achieved. Every day that the Lord wakes me up, I have another day of mercy, another day to be a blessing to others and not just for me. I pray that I can be a Godly role model for children and an example for the lost souls out there. With God's help and His love for me, I can do anything. I trust You my God, my Father, my Friend, and my Protector.

I Corinthians Chapter 16 Verse 13,

Watch ye, stand fast in the faith, quit you like me, be strong.

I BELONG TO YOU

I was Created from **You**

And Created for **You**

From the Dust, I came,

And the Dust, I Shall Return

Your Love is so Tangible

When I Wake up in the Morning,

I thank **You** for Another Day

Crying to Weeping in the Night

Leads me to Joy in the Morning

I look for a Realm to Belong too

How Can I Fit In?

My Season is Near,

I CAN FEEL IT

You've given me Favor

In my Days of Trials and Obstacles

Why do I Complain
When things don't look Bright?

The Price **You** Paid for me
I know I could NEVER Endure
My life is My Responsibility
It has the Power to Make Choices

I Choose to Live for **You**
Or I Choose to Die without **You**

LORD I ASK DO I BELONG TO YOU?

Your Answer is
YOU'VE ALWAYS BELONG TO ME,
For I've called You by Name

CHAPTER 7

Down in the Valley

The number 7 is a very significant number. This number means complete in God's Word. I'm being blessed right now because I'm completing a goal today March 27, 2018, which is my book. This chapter is to let me know the trials and tribulations are here for me to grow in wisdom and faith to help others.

During the month of May, I had my yearly mammogram done. The same day I had this done, the hospital called me because something was on the breast. I was in shock for a few seconds, then I broke out in tears for a few minutes. The next thing I did was I called on Jesus, my Lord and Savior for strength. Then I remembered my favorite scripture *Proverbs Chapter 3 Verse 5-6*. That scripture caused me to look at the situation differently and I praised God for being there for me.

That Friday I went to the breast center and had another mammogram and they found calcium clusters in my left breast. Even though I'm a young 48-year-old woman, I can produce breast milk and get pregnant. I had a biopsy done and a pre-cancer cell was removed. My God made sure this cell was caught before it became cancerous. There's a clip in my breast on the spot where the clusters are. This will help keep an eye on the area where the calcium clusters are incased another pre-cancer cell pops up. So, you never know what life will bring you just trust your Heavenly Father, He will get you through.

Having gone through this my things are not over yet. I've been having pain in my left arm for a while now. The pain started around 2005. The doctor thought it was a pinched nerve, but that wasn't the correct diagnosis.

In fact, the doctor could not find out why my arm was hurting. The pain stopped and I thought I was okay until a month later.

In July 2009, the pain came back so I went to another neurologist. The neurologist recommended that I have an MRI on my neck to see if I had a bad disk in my neck. The results of the MRI of my neck will be in soon, so keep reading to find out the outcome.

To those who read this book, think about how you are blessed every day. The Spirit of God wakes you up, not the alarm clock. Readers you may be saying, if God loves me so much why am I going through all the trials and tribulations in my life. God wants you to turn to Him for strength and more faith in Him. When you are healed from whatever you're going through, God wants to get the glory, so you can be a better witness for Him. I am a witness to what God can do for me and others in my life. Jesus is my source for strength, courage, and hope for a better brighter life here on earth. My hope is I will help others in life and share my life with my male soulmate to love, be in love with him, and cherish him for the rest of my days here on earth.

Oh, regarding the neck MRI results, I have three herniated disks in my back around my spine. The neurologist recommended that I get surgery. My Spirit told me no, therefore, I'm doing therapy instead. So, you see after all the storms I've been through, I still trust my Spirit and my Daddy God.

II Corinthians Chapter 1 Verse 3-4:

Blessed be the God and Father of our Lord Jesus Christ, the Father of mercies and God of all comfort; who comforts us in All our tribulation, that we may be able to comfort those who are in any trouble, With the comfort with which we ourselves Are comforted by God.

DOWN IN THE VALLEY

How do I look Above?

When I've Been **DOWN** for So Long?

Is Life just FULL of Rejection, Turmoil?

OR is there Hope on the Other Side?

Why do you Despise me?

Why don't you Love me?

Could it be the way I Look, the way I Talk?

OR is it because I Love you with Sincerity from the Heart?

I am just a little Girl who wanted to be Loved,

To Laugh and be Filled with Joy

Now, that I am a Woman

You still HAVEN'T Heard me

I Guess you just Choose to NOT Listen

Just Remember,

I will ALWAYS Love you UNTIL I can't Love NO MORE

CHAPTER 8

Prosperity

Through the storms of life; now I have the victory that my God said I would have if I just keep the faith and trust in my God's Word. Sometimes we as people that know the Lord and worship Him in prayer and praise, think that the trivial things that God does for us have no big meaning. But, I want to set the record straight for those who think like this. I sometimes use to think that trivial things meant nothing because the blessings were small, but Praise God I was wrong because little things were really big blessings from God. There are so many things I can thank God for, but it would take me a lifetime to write them all down.

As I sit here typing this last chapter a few things come to mind. I never understood the real meaning of supernatural blessings, but I have had a few take place in my life. About a year ago I needed $600 to take care of some debt and I didn't have anywhere to get it from. My mother was no longer here so, I had to work this out on my own.

Two weeks went by and there was a check in the mail for $500. The check came from a source that I never thought about, but this is what a supernatural blessing means when you serve the Lord with love, be honest with yourself in life, and not be a phony person or Christian. Even though I needed $600, the $500 took care of all the debt I needed to take care of.

In today's world, God is waiting for more of His children to come unto Him and receive the blessings He has for them. Through my walk with God, I was still not making good choices in life. I took out a loan when I knew that was against God's Word. It says, be a lender, not a borrower. I had to learn the hard way; thank God, I learned while I was still young and still here on this earth to receive my blessings.

I grow every day in the Lord and I have learned so much more about God's Word. The Book of Proverbs is the "Book of Wisdom" for us to get the knowledge we need as people to grow and have blessings beyond our understanding. I have God in my heart and that is the reason I'm where I am now in my life the year of 2018. I always keep God first in everything I do, meaning, before my future husband, my children, my family, and my business which brings me income, or anything else in this world He is first.

God's Word is the blueprint for me to love one another, even love the people who have treated me wrong, and who has put me down as a person. The Bible was designed for us to love each other, have life, and have life more abundantly. It's not all about big houses or being rich; it's about having those things to be a blessing to others. I vowed to God years ago that when I make my millions, yes, I said millions; it will not only be a blessing to me and my house, but to be a blessing to others in need.

I know my purpose here on this earth is to help children know how to have the life God has for them. My purpose is to share my life story to those that are hurting, and they can call me a friend. Also, I will be there for them in Spirit and in truth. I know I can't change anyone, but I can show them love, give them the tools they need to love themselves, and to prosper. In addition, to have joy and peace that God has given me.

In 2012, was a test year for me, it was a year that I never want to go through again. It was so hard paying my bills and being a single parent. I know things were difficult because of my disobedience to God's Word. His Word taught me never to take a loan out and never live beyond your means.

Today in 2018, I can say I learned my lesson. Now, I'm seeing the fruits of my labor, not just from 2012, but from all my adult life. My undying faith, my complete trust, having patience, and studying God's Word over the years has and continues to help me to reap my harvest. Now, it's not all coming at once, but it's coming in the way that will keep me on track with my faith until the flood of blessings comes to my house.

I received another supernatural blessing in June 2013, a debt was paid off without me giving any money to pay it off. In September the same year, again I received a check from a source that I wasn't expecting. Praise God in October that I found money at a time I needed it.

In March 2017, I'm just amazed what God did for me. I learned about sowing seed at my church. I sowed $10 one Sunday and within two weeks I received a check for $1000; I gave God all the glory and praise. God is showing me to get ready for a blessing that will have me to pass out (smile).

I write this to show you when you give your life and have a real and pure relationship with God from the heart, things like this can happen to you and beyond. This is what God wants for His children that accepts His Son into their hearts and life of Jesus Christ.

Keep in mind, God looks on the inside and not on the outside. Don't ever think you can fool God by thinking, well, I will come to Him, so I can get something; that's not what God is for. God wants you to love Him first, keep Him first in your life, and change your heart to love one another and your enemies. Then all these things shall be added unto you. Study His Word, mediate on it every day, and worship Him in Spirit and in truth. God looks for us to come to Him with our whole heart and faith. In today's world, it can be hard sometimes, but with Jesus, your heavy load of life can be easy if you just turn it over to Him!!!

In concluding this chapter, I can look back on where God has brought me from. Thank You, God for keeping me alive from molestation, being bullied, raped, beaten by so-called friends, choked by an ex-boyfriend which I almost died, attacked in front of a school at the age of 12, cheated on and abused by my ex-husband. I tell this story because I want anyone who reads my book to know that God brought me through this life of hurt, therefore, He can bring anyone through their trials and tribulations!!! I wanted to commit suicide many times, but the Holy Spirit kept speaking to me because God has a purpose for my life here on this earth.

As I sit here crying looking back over my life, I thank God for keeping me here and allowing me to realize that He has put a gift in me and He wants me to complete in me what He started. I give glory and praise to my God and my Savior Jesus Christ!!!

Speak this and keep the faith, my season's coming around again. Purpose is a journey and seasons are not always good.

Are you in a place in your life where even your dreams believe?

A Season is Nothing but an Opportunity!!!

Proverbs Chapter 3 Verse 5-6

Jeremiah Chapter 29 Verse 11-15

PROSPERITY

OH, the Dawn of Day,

I wake up to the Light,

Sun So Bright

Able to Speak, Able to Pray

Is Today the Beginning of my Life?

Have I Agonized over my Goals?

Wondering what would come to Pass

OH, how I wish Life was Easier

To receive **PROSPERITY**

Am I Wishing on a Star?

Am I Diluting myself?

Do I have what it Takes to Prosper?

What is Really the Meaning of **PROSPERITY?**

Is it about Things, Money,

The right kind of People you are Around?

NO PROSPERITY is Helping Mankind

People who are Struggling within Themselves
Helping those in Need

We Prosper when we Listen to other people's Needs
And Lend our Helping Hand

Helping one another to Get what they Want
Our Reward at the End
Will Be So Great

INSPIRATIONAL POETRY

A DREAMER

DREAMS, DREAMS,

Oh, How Wonderful are **MY DREAMS**

Black and White, Blue or Red. . .

No matter what Color **MY DREAMS** are,

What a Beautiful **DREAM**

I see a big House on Top of the Hill,

With Flowers Blooming all Around

I see a Colorful Rainbow in the Sky,

OH, what a Beautiful Sight to See

Gods Promises to be

With the World at War and Rage

With Bombs and Guns

People are so Afraid!

Babies Crying, Children Dying,

But still, I am **A DREAMER**

In the Midst of the Day,

There is Laughter

There may be Sorrow,

Yet, **I DREAM** for Tomorrow

To **DREAM** is to Believe,

To Vision, You'll Receive

DREAMER I AM. . .

VISIONS I SEE. . .

A DREAMER I WILL BE

GROWING UP LIKE THIS AS A CHILD

GROWING UP LIKE THIS AS A CHILD,
Shouldn't happen to **ANY CHILD**

Today in 2017 there are so many **CHILDREN**
GROWING UP without a Father in the Home,
And no Mentor or a real Role Model
To help that Single Parent

Love is very Important
To a **CHILD'S DEVELOPMENT** in Life
Without Love, we will make Bad Choices
And Head Down the WRONG Path in Life

I know some Obstacles and Challenges
Are to Help Make Us Stronger,
But for a young girl or boy
I feel this **SHOULD HAPPEN** Later in Life

THE LITTLE BOY

Ten Little Fingers,

Ten Little Toes

A Handsome **BABY BOY** is Born

Big Bright Eyes

Shining Bright Skin. . .

So Soft, Oh what a Delight

Months gone by, Growing like a Weed,

Bouncing Up and Down on Grandmoms Knee

He Laughs when he's Tickled

And his Eyes Shine up like the Sun

A Handsome **LITTLE BOY** just Begun

Swinging in the Trees Chattering away,

Angels surround him Protecting him from the Bees

Mommy, Daddy look at me

He says Swinging High Happy as can be

Years have gone by, **LITTLE BOY** NO MORE,

All grown up Handsome has can be

Mommy and Daddy Don't Cry

That **LITTLE BOY** is still Alive

I may be Grown and Now a Man,

But in my Heart,

I'm still **YOUR LITTLE BOY**

THE LITTLE GIRL

Ten Little Toes,

Ten Little Fingers

A Beautiful **Baby GIRL**

Big bright Eyes shining Bright,

Skin So Soft, Oh what a Delight

Months gone by, Growing like a Weed,

Bouncing up and down

On Grand Daddy's Knee

She Laughs when she's Tickled,

And her Eyes Shine Up like the Sun

A Beautiful **LITTLE GIRL** just Begun

Swinging in the Trees, Chattering away,

Angels surround her, Protecting her from the Bees

Mommy, Daddy look at me she says,

Swinging high happy as can be

Years have Gone by,

LITTLE GIRL no More,

All grown up Beautiful to See

Mommy and Daddy DON'T Cry,

That **LITTLE GIRL** is still Alive

I may be Grown and Now a Woman,

But in my Heart,

I AM STILL YOUR LITTLE GIRL

FATHER'S DAY

FATHERS are Created from Above,

A FATHER'S Love is like the Sun,

That Lights up the Day

His Love is like a Rainbow

That Appears AFTER the Rain

His Promise to his Children

Will ALWAYS Remain the Same

The Love of **A FATHER** HEALS a Broken Heart

Through his Faith he receives from the Start

The Love of **A FATHER** is a Gift from God

That a child Feels the Gift

That lights up a child's face from Ear to Ear

A FATHER treats his children with Respect and Care,

And Hopes their Dreams Blossom in mid-air

My FATHER stands Proud and Strong,

For his Love is Everlasting and Long

WHO CAN DEFINE A MAN?

A MAN was created in God's image;
CAN A MAN be like God?

Will we ever know the Answer?

CAN A MAN love a Woman,
The way God loves a Woman?

I ask, **DOES A MAN** respect a Woman?
DOES A MAN cherish a Woman, God does?

DOES A MAN take on the Role of a Father,
Or is he just a Dad?

DOES A MAN grab a Woman out of Anger or Rage
Or does he Grab her and Hold her
With Compassion and Love?

God holds a Woman with Compassion and Love

CAN A MAN be like God?

Do you know the Answer?

If you know God, you know the Answer

WHO CAN DEFINE A MAN?

Robin D. Johnson

WHO CAN DEFINE A WOMAN?

A WOMAN was Created from Heaven Above,

Thru a man from Gods Love

DOES A WOMAN a Mother to you and me?

A WOMAN carries herself with Dignity and Grace,

With Favor to the Human Race

She smiles when Times are Hard,

She cares for her Young and Supports her Old

She knows when to Cry and when to Laugh,

She knows when to Fall on her Knees and Pray

When her children have gone Astray

Her Heart is of Gold that you CAN'T See,

Her face Glows with Love

That lightens up the Sea

A WOMAN'S Beauty is seen

With the Spiritual Eye,

For **A WOMAN'S** Love is

Long Lasting not just 9 to 5

WOMEN Stand Strong and be Proud,

For your Love WILL Shine

Until the End of Time

Robin D. Johnson

A HUSBAND, A WIFE

HUSBAND So Strong and Handsome,
A Provider God made you to be
Standing Firm in Doing Well,
For his **WIFE** and Family

Your Spirit and Love comes from Above,
With a Smile that Lights Up the Sky
You Hold me with Tender Loving Care,
And Shower me with Kisses, Oh So Sweet

When Challenges enter into my Day. . .
To Rob me of my Joy,
You say my Darling **WIFE** take My Hand. . .
For your Challenges are Now Set Free

MY WIFE, When I Look at you
I see a Beautiful Woman
Your Face Glows when you Smile,
Your Inner Beauty Shines through

Your Laughter Lights up the Room

A Helper you are Sent from God Above

A HUSBAND'S Love is Extraordinary,

A WIFE'S love is Complete. . .

Two have become One,

With Love that has just Begun

Robin D. Johnson

MY LOVE

Another day is Here and it's ONLY just Begun

The Sun is Shining, Birds are Singing,

LOVE is in the Air

MY LOVE you have Showered me with Gifts

That have Beautified My Life

And Enhances **MY LOVE** for you

I am NEVER alone, you are ALWAYS there

In the morning you Communicate with me,

Laugh with me and even sometimes Cry with me,

But you are ALWAYS there for me

When days seem so Overwhelming,

You take My Hand and say,

Beloved DON'T be Dismayed

For LOVE will Bring you through

MY LOVE,

You are Awesome and Beautiful

Inside and Out

You have given your Life for me

So, my life will be Free

The Precious Diamond you are lights up my Face

Strong hands you have when I am Embraced

Your Love is here to Stay, even if I go Astray

So, remember these Words. . .

Love is like a Flower that Grows every day,

That Showers me with Smelling Savory

Throughout the Day

NATURAL LOVE, SPIRITUAL LOVE

What God has joined together,
Let No Man Put Asunder!

Love is like a Flower,
It Blossoms at any given moment
SPIRITUAL LOVE blossoms
At the Beginning of Time

NATURAL LOVE can fade away
At the Twinkle of an Eye

SPIRITUAL LOVE will never fade away.
NATURAL LOVE that joins a
Woman and Man WILL Drift away

But a Marriage joined by God
WILL Create Everlasting Rainbows

My Darling,

Our Love is Skin-Deep like the Oceans

Our Souls are Bonded with God

God created Man,

And Woman for Man

We Are Now One!

GIRLFRIEND

A Friend in the Good times,

Friend in the Bad times

Out in the Field on a Hot Sunny Day,

Chatting with My **GIRLFRIEND**

To Pass the Time away

What is a **GIRLFRIEND?**

Someone to Laugh with, Someone to Cry with,

Or just sitting around Exchanging Old Family Recipes

GIRLFRIENDS,

When I'm Hungry will you Feed me?

When I'm Thirsty will you Give Me Drink?

When life Throws a Curve and Circumstances arises,

That is Hard to Endure

Would the Door of Heart be Open

OR Would I be Ignored?

WHAT IS A FRIEND?

You may say you are **A FRIEND** to the end;

The End is not near, Yet **NO FRIEND** is Near

My name you tried to Destroy,

My Kindness you've used to Clean the Floor;

You called me when in Need, to Gossip or to Mislead

Acquaintance I have,

But **FRIENDS** are No Where to be Found

A FRIEND can make you Laugh,

A FRIEND can make you cry Tears for Joy

A TRUE FRIEND will always be Near,

Even when there is some Fear

Are you **A FRIEND** or Space to be Filled?

I know **A TRUE FRIEND**

That will ALWAYS be Near

I need not to mention His Name,

BECAUSE HE'S ALWAYS NEAR

Robin D. Johnson

PEACE

The Air is Crisp,

The Trees are Blooming

Love is in the Air. . .

As I Walk Down the Road

I look Around and what do I Feel?

NO PEACE I say is Near

Gangs are Emerging,

Drugs are Destroying our Young

When will the World have **PEACE?**

Our young men are Fighting in Wars

Dying for Others,

But yet I see NO Remorse

Do we as People Even Care

That there is **NO PEACE** in the World?

Children are Crying

People are Dying

But how do I really Feel?

Is there **PEACE** anywhere?

I am a young lady who Cares

Do you See what I See?

Do you Feel what I Feel?

Is the World So Blind?

That they can't see the

Devastation around them?

Are you Closing your Eyes to the Truth?

Do you care that the Evilness

That's taking over our youth?

Mothers where is your Love for your Children,

Fathers, why do you leave Home So Soon?

Do We Care?

My God, what went Wrong?
The Beginning was so Beautiful...
But What is the End for Us?

RESPECT

Honor I have Esteemed I Uphold

Humble to Thee, Faithfulness You Adore

Returned to me Repaid to me,

My Peace and Quietness

Guide me Thru the Storms

That Darkness as Endured for Deliverance

Must become a Time I will Enjoy

RESPECT, I must have to Inspire Myself

Thanks, Be unto You

My Life Has Become a New

Light Shines around my Home,

Glowing to No End

Peace is Still,

Life is Complete

MY BROTHER WHY KILL ANOTHER?

MY BROTHER So Fine,

Why Spend your Time to Kill

Another of your **BROTHER'S?**

Why So Angry?

Why So Bitter?

WHY KILL ANOTHER?

Our Race has come a Mighty Long Way

Why have you Gone Astray?

Where's the Love?

Where's the Peace?

Can you see the Slavery Mentality?

It just won't Let you be Free

Strive, Hate. . .

Don't make that Mistake

BROTHERHOOD is the Way,

Society shares in Brutality

Do you Agree that our **BROTHER'S** are not Free?

My BROTHER, Look into your Mind

What do you See?

Are you in Bondage?

Is your Mind Alert?

Do you see what I See?

MY BROTHER, WHY KILL ANOTHER?

Our Children are Dying,

Our Race is Becoming Instinct

In the Beginning, God created Man,

Let's take a Stand and Complete God's Plan

Love One Another,

NOT KILL ONE ANOTHER

Robin D. Johnson

SOUL BROTHER

SOUL BROTHER,
SOUL BROTHER,
What that means to me

We've Walked together, Talked together,
How Sweet life can be?
Promises you made you never Broke

Your word is Filling with Truth that Runs like Water
When your days were Full of Test
And Daily Tasks were Hard,
You stepped in and lighten the Burdens from Afar

My Brother other So Fine you are
And Awesome you have Become
You Light up my Life with your Love
Till all My Work has been Done

SOUL BROTHER
We have been through many Storms
Summer time, winter time, fall, and spring

Each time you were there to Help me have Peace

I love you **SOUL BROTHER** with every Breath I take

May people come to Know you and Love you

JUST AS I DO

SATISFIES

I Cried out to You, Have Mercy on Me

My Time is Short, My Life is in Your Hands

I'm NOT Ashamed of My Past

Or the Wicked Things that TRY to Destroy me

My Soul is Preserve to Glorify You

SATISFACTION goes Deep Down

In my Heart, Body, and Soul

I can be **SATISFIED** in my Mourning

And **SATISFIED** in My Goodness

Strength I have in You,

Supplication You Hear when I Pray

Behold I will Surpass the Enemy

That Surrounds me with Fear

For my Life is **SATISFIED**

Knowing You Are Near

LIVE FOR TODAY

In the Midst of the Day, all is Well

Down on My Knees,

I look to the Lord with Admiration,

To thank Him for **ANOTHER DAY** of Mercy

Struggles I have just a Few,

But the Wisdom I have will get me Through

Frustration sometimes Attacks my Soul,

But a Smile on My Face,

Keeps the Frustration from ever being Told

Life is So Short, one might say,

For tomorrow Dawns a **NEW DAY**

May your **DAYS** be Filled

With Love and Kindness,

Especially to One Another

Don't Argue or Yell with a Face of a Frown

You are Special and Loved

We are Kings & Queens from Above

CHRISTIAN, I AM, CHRISTIAN, I WILL BE

At the Beginning of Time,

You knew What I would Be

Accomplishments You Did See

Chosen I became to Fulfill Your Plans

My true Destiny,

In the Palm of Your Hands

Life is Short I use to Think,

But Living a **CHRISTIAN LIFE** is, Oh So Sweet

Eternity, I shall Have,

A Kingdom So Divine,

With Jesus, the Head of me

I started this **CHRISTIAN RACE** so long ago,

Not knowing the Course, I would be on,

Just knowing at the End, a just Reward I WILL Own

THE PRECIOUS GIFT

What is a **PRECIOUS GIFT?**

A Woman is a Gift from God to Man

A Man is a **GIFT** to a Woman from God

But what is the **PRECIOUS GIFT** from God?

The sound of Laughter is a **GIFT,**

The Warmth from the Sun

That God provides is a **GIFT**

The Bright Light from the Moon

That Shines at Night is a **GIFT**

Love is a **UNCONDITIONAL GIFT,**

Being able to Smile is a **GIFT**

The **GIFT** that will ENHANCE your Life

Is carried by a Woman for 9 months

Wrap these **GIFTS** into One,

And you will find the **PRECIOUS GIFT!**

The **GIFT** of a Child is the **PRECIOUS GIFT!**

LOOK TO THE HILLS

LOOK TO THE HILLS

From Whence Cometh My Help

I will Lift up My Eyes

HILLS are so hard to Climb

You are Half Way there

And you CAN'T seem to Reach the Top

Sometimes you Fall Back to the Bottom

And you have to Start Over Again

Frustration sets in,

Despair, that isn't Fair

Still you KEEP Climbing that **HILL**

When you Stop and Look

At the **HILLS** you have to Climb,

You wonder if it's Worth the Time

Not knowing what you'll Do,

Or what lies at the End

All you know is the Victory you will have

When you Reach the Top

Life is like a **HILL**,

You're Climbing to Reach

Your Goals and Desires in Life,

But you can't seem to reach the Top of the **HILL**

WITH GOD ALL THINGS ARE POSSIBLE

Remember, the **HILL** is just an Obstacle,

Continue to Strive for the Prize

And Press Towards the Goal

RESTORED

Oh Lord, My Strength, My Redeemer

My Hope, My God

WHAT HAVE I DONE?

Have I Lost My Life?

Can My Past be **RESTORED?**

What is Life really about?

Have I given You My Life Completely?

Or am I just Passing by?

My Future has been Sown

Oh Lord, My Life has been **RESTORED**

With Faith, Love, and Hope

Perseverance guides My Future to be Fulfilled

Today I am **RESTORED**

And I SHALL Declare Victory

My Soul has been **RESTORED!**

YESTERDAY IS GONE

As a New Day Arises,

YESTERDAY IS GONE

I look back at My Past and say, So Long

I've come from a Mighty Long Way able to say,

Happy I am in this Life Today

As I sit here on a Cool Night

I look at the Stars Above,

I plan for My Future

Because **YESTERDAY IS GONE**

My Past I lived in Darkness

Not knowing the Truth,

What the Lord had in Store for My Youth

Dreams can be Achieved,

Visions are Real,

THANK GOD ALMIGHTY I AM STILL HERE!

I Cultivate My Mind

To Achieve at this Time,

To Live for Today,

For Tomorrow SHALL be Mine

The Past is Thrown into the Sea,

And My Life has been Set Free

For Success is just around the Bend,

OH, THANK HEAVENS, I CAN LIVE AGAIN

I am an Eagle Soaring High,

To Land among the Stars

In a Twinkle of an Eye

Past Dreams are Gone,

Today's Dreams are Real

YESTERDAY IS GONE,

TODAY, I AM STILL HERE!

ABOUT THE AUTHOR

Robin D. Johnson was born in Wilmington, Delaware on June 25, 1961. She now resides in New Castle, Delaware. Robin is the mother of two beautiful and blessed children, Samuel E. Davis Jr., and Tamera D. Davis. In addition, she's a proud Nana of one grandson and one granddaughter.

Robin's goal and dreams in life are to help those in need when she can. One of her passions is to help our children here in Delaware and one day with God's help, she plans to assist children all over the world.

Robin accepted Jesus Christ in her life as her Lord and Savior at the early age of 26 and now loves the Lord so adequately. She shares God's love by sharing her love among others. During her walk with Christ, she was the president of the youth ministry at her former church in the 1990's. She also sang in the church choir and helped her mother in Sunday school.

Robin is a member of Bethany Baptist Church located in Lindenwold, New Jersey, under the awesome teachings of Bishop David G. Evans. She loves this fellowship and plans to continue worshiping there until she leaves this earth.

With the love of God in her life, she is very family oriented and loves her family, even those she does not know well. In Robin's walk with Christ; she has learned that God is love and receiving His grace has helped her become the woman she is today. One thing Robin does know is that she's not perfect, but her heart is right because of the love of Jesus.

Robin was raised by a single mother who is now no longer here on earth. Her mother was blessed because she had Christ in her life too. Robin said her mother, Dorothy gave of her heart, her time, her true love for children, and could never say no to anyone in need if she could help them.

One thing Robin can say is that her mother blessed her by keeping her in God's house from an infant to an adult. Without God and Jesus Christ in her life to guide her, she feels she would have been dead a long time ago. Therefore, being transformed by the renewing of her mind, learning God's Word and wisdom every day, keeps her healthy, trusting, and keeping the faith. Even when life seems unfair. She continues to pray daily that her goals and dreams in this life come to pass.

Robin was blessed 17-years-ago to work from home by helping people and families. She is an entrepreneur/business owner and is an Independent Associate with Legal Shield Corporation.

Robin has recently designed an app and hopes to have it on the market soon. This is her first book which she is extremely proud. Robin, also became a contractor with the Vanguard Emergency Management and works for FEMA when there was a disaster.

Being a part of Bethany Baptist Church, Robin volunteers often to help those less fortunate. One thing about Robin, if she has a few dollars on her and sees a homeless person, she will give her last dollar to them. Giving makes her feel great!!! Also, Robin will be assisting her church with the Prison Ministry. In addition, Robin is geared to helping children in need to become successful.

Now, she is a single mother, but believes God that she will one day soon have the man of her dreams to become her husband. She always said that her Boaz, which will be her soul-mate is on his way.

Her favorite scripture is Proverbs Chapter 3 Verses 5-6. In these trying times, Robin continues to trust God even thou some days things get rough. But no matter what happens, her heart and faith won't let her give up. In fact, everything about her is a testament of how she lives her life because of her faithful relationship with God and her Savior Jesus Christ!!! The Holy Spirit guides her steps daily. Most importantly, helps her to Dream Big, Trust God, Have Faith, Sow Seeds in God's Word, and Watch the Move of God!!!

www.ingramcontent.com/pod-product-compliance
Lightning Source LLC
Chambersburg PA
CBHW050443010526
44118CB00013B/1661